TAKE A WILD GUESS . . .

WHY IS THIS SAND
DUNE HUMMING?

WHY DOESN'T THIS CAT
HAVE ANY HAIR?

WHAT FLIES 500 MILES
PER HOUR—15 FEET OFF
THE GROUND?

WHAT DENTED THIS CAR?

IF YOU DON'T KNOW ANY OF THE
WEIRD-BUT-TRUE ANSWERS TO THESE
QUESTIONS, RELAX! YOU'RE ABOUT TO
HAVE FUN FINDING OUT.

CONTENTS

PEOPLE & CUSTOMS

FOR YEARS, SOME OF THE WORLD'S MOST FAMOUS BRAINS HAVE BEEN STORED IN LABORATORIES SO THAT ONE DAY SCIENTISTS COULD STUDY THEM. THE TROUBLE IS, SCIENTISTS AREN'T SURE IF IT'S THE GRAY MATTER THAT MAKES THE BRAIN SPECIAL—OR THE CHEMICALS IN THE BRAIN, WHICH DECAY WHEN A PERSON DIES.

SLICED... OR CUBED!!

ALBERT EINSTEIN

AT LAST REPORT, THE 20TH CENTURY'S MOST BRILLIANT SCIENTIFIC BRAIN FLOATS IN TWO PICKLING JARS IN THE LAWRENCE, KANSAS, APARTMENT OF DR. THOMAS HARVEY—THE PHYSICIAN WHO REMOVED IT AFTER EINSTEIN DIED IN 1955. DR. HARVEY CUT THE BRAIN INTO DOZENS OF CUBES AND HUNDREDS OF SLICES, SOME OF WHICH HE SENT TO PROMINENT BRAIN RESEARCHERS. THE REST HE KEPT AND TOOK WITH HIM WHEN HE LATER MOVED AND RETIRED. SO FAR, NONE OF THE RESEARCHERS HAS REPORTED ANYTHING MIND-BOGGLING.

VLADIMIR ILYICH LENIN

WHEN THE FATHER OF SOVIET COMMUNISM DIED IN 1924, SCIENTISTS REMOVED HIS BRAIN AND CUT IT INTO 31,000 SLICES. THEY STORED THE SLICES ON SLIDES AT THE MOSCOW BRAIN INSTITUTE, WHICH WAS SET UP TO STUDY THE BRAINS OF PROMINENT SOVIET CITIZENS. AFTER THE SOVIET UNION COLLAPSED IN 1991, THE SECRET FINDINGS ON LENIN'S BRAIN WERE RELEASED: IT WAS PRETTY AVERAGE.

WALT WHITMAN

AFTER HIS DEATH IN 1892, POET WALT WHITMAN'S BRAIN WAS KEPT IN A JAR AT THE WISTAR INSTITUTE AT THE UNIVERSITY OF PENNSYLVANIA, WHICH ONCE HOUSED MORE THAN 200 BRAINS. BUT A NUMBER OF YEARS AGO, A LABORATORY WORKER DROPPED WHITMAN'S BRAIN ON THE FLOOR, AND IT HAD TO BE THROWN AWAY.

IN JAPAN, SOME PEOPLE HOLD FUNERALS FOR EVERYDAY THINGS THAT HAVE BROKEN. THE CEREMONIES, CALLED *KUYŌ*, HONOR THE OBJECTS FOR THEIR FAITHFUL SERVICE.

A FUNERAL FOR BROKEN DOLLS TAKES PLACE EACH YEAR IN KYOTO. A BUDDHIST PRIEST CHANTS THE PRAYER FOR THE DEAD, THEN THE DOLLS ARE CREMATED.

EACH WINTER, TAILORS AND KIMONO MAKERS GATHER OLD SEWING NEEDLES AND STICK THEM IN A PIECE OF TOFU (BEAN CURD) TO GIVE THEM A SOFT RESTING PLACE. THEN THEY SAY A PRAYER TO COMFORT THE NEEDLES' SPIRITS.

EVEN MODERN OBJECTS ARE SOMETIMES MOURNED. IN 1990 ENGINEERS FROM SEVERAL ELECTRONICS FIRMS HELD A FUNERAL FOR WORN-OUT HIGH-TECH PARTS. AT A 400-YEAR-OLD BUDDHIST TEMPLE IN TOKYO, THEY PILED UP OLD COMPUTER CHIPS, VCR RECORDING HEADS, CAMERA LENSES, AND OTHER OUTDATED COMPONENTS. AFTER RECITING A PRAYER, THEY GATHERED OUTSIDE TO BURN PICTURES OF THE OBJECTS. (BURNING THE OBJECTS THEMSELVES WOULD HAVE CAUSED AIR POLLUTION.)

EVERY ONCE IN A WHILE, PEOPLE ARE BORN WITH MORE THAN THE USUAL NUMBER OF BODY PARTS. HERE ARE SOME EXTRA-SPECIAL EXAMPLES.

THE MALE MEMBERS OF THIS MEXICAN FAMILY HAVE INCH-LONG HAIR COVERING THEIR FACES AND SHOULDERS. THE GIRLS AND WOMEN ARE ALSO PRETTY HAIRY, BUT NOT AS MUCH. SCIENTISTS THINK THE TRAIT IS CAUSED BY A GENE FROM THE DISTANT PAST WHEN EVERYONE WAS COVERED WITH HAIR. THIS GENE IS NORMALLY SWITCHED OFF, BUT IN THIS FAMILY IT WAS ACCIDENTALLY SWITCHED ON. ONLY ABOUT 50 SUCH CASES HAVE EVER BEEN REPORTED.

IN ONE LARGE TURKISH FAMILY IT'S NORMAL TO HAVE 6 FINGERS ON EACH HAND AND 6 TOES ON EACH FOOT. NOBODY MAKES A BIG DEAL ABOUT IT, AND THE EXTRA DIGITS DON'T SEEM TO GET IN THE WAY. RESEARCHERS THINK THE TRAIT IS A GENETIC MUTATION, WHICH HAS SO FAR BEEN PASSED DOWN THROUGH 7 GENERATIONS.

IT'S ALSO EXTREMELY RARE, BUT SOME BABIES ARE BORN WITH A SHORT TAIL THAT THEY CAN MOVE FROM SIDE TO SIDE. THE TAIL HAS NO BONES. IT IS ALMOST ALWAYS CUT OFF BY DOCTORS, BUT IF LEFT ON, IT WOULD DEVELOP WITH THE BABY'S BODY AND MIGHT EVEN GROW HAIR. ACTUALLY, EVERYBODY HAS A TAIL FOR A WHILE WHEN THEY ARE DEVELOPING INSIDE THEIR MOTHER'S WOMB. BIOLOGISTS THINK THAT A FEW PEOPLE JUST NEVER LOSE THEIRS.

PEOPLE IN OTHER CULTURES
SOMETIMES SUFFER FROM
ILLNESSES THAT A DOCTOR
TRAINED IN WESTERN MEDICINE
MIGHT CALL IMAGINARY. BUT
TO THEM, THE DISEASES ARE
VERY REAL. SEE IF YOU HAVE EVER
HAD ANY OF THESE COMPLAINTS.

ALIEN AILMENTS

DO YOU FEEL AS IF YOUR SOUL HAS
BEEN FRIGHTENED OUT OF YOUR
BODY? IN LATIN AMERICA YOU'D HAVE
SUSTO.

DO YOU (A) SULK AND THEN (B) SUDDENLY DO VIOLENT THINGS? YOU MIGHT HAVE THE CONDITION KNOWN AS AMOK IN MALAYSIA.

HAVE YOU EVER SPENT A HALF HOUR SCREAMING AND BEING VIOLENT, THEN GONE INTO A SHORT COMA? THE INUIT WOULD SAY YOU'VE HAD AN ATTACK OF PIBLOKTOQ.

ARE YOU ALWAYS WORRIED ABOUT DEATH, AND DO YOU FREQUENTLY FAINT AND HAVE BAD DREAMS? NATIVE AMERICANS WOULD SAY YOU HAD GHOST SICKNESS.

DO YOU BECOME EXTREMELY UPSET AND ATTACK PEOPLE, YET FEEL CONFUSED? HAITIANS AND EAST AFRICANS WOULD SUSPECT BOUFÉE DELIRANTE.

ARE YOU EXTREMELY WORRIED THAT YOUR BODILY FUNCTIONS WILL OFFEND OTHER PEOPLE? IN JAPAN YOU'D ALMOST CERTAINLY HAVE TAIJIN KYOFUSHO.

9

ACCORDING TO CHINESE TRADITION, BAD LUCK CAN STRIKE IF YOUR HOME, BUSINESS, OR FAMILY TOMB IS IN THE WRONG PLACE. MANY CHINESE RELY ON THE SYSTEM CALLED *FENG SHUI* (PRONOUNCED **FENG**-SHWAY) TO DETERMINE THE LUCKIEST PLACES TO PUT THINGS. *FENG SHUI* MEANS "WIND AND WATER" IN CHINESE, BECAUSE THE SYSTEM SEEKS HARMONY WITH NATURAL FORCES.

HERE ARE SOME EXAMPLES OF BAD AND *GOOD FENG SHUI*.

BAD *FENG SHUI*

• TOP OF HILL (WINDY—LUCK AND MONEY COULD ROLL OUT THE DOOR)

• OVERHANGING ROCK (COULD FALL ON YOU)

• STRAIGHT DRIVEWAY AT BOTTOM OF HILL (CAN SEND "KILLING" FORCES TOWARD HOUSE)

GOOD *FENG SHUI*

•HOUSE HALFWAY UP SOUTH-FACING SLOPE
(LESS WINDY THAN TOP; SUNNY IN WINTER)

•VIEW OF WATER (LIFE-GIVING FORCE)

•WINDING DRIVEWAY (FOOLS DEMONS, WHICH FLY IN
STRAIGHT LINES)

IF YOU THINK YOUR HOUSE HAS BAD *FENG SHUI*, YOU
CAN HIRE A *FENG SHUI* EXPERT TO LOOK AROUND
YOUR HOUSE FOR PLACES THAT ATTRACT BAD LUCK.
DEPENDING ON YOUR HOME'S LAYOUT AND LOCATION,
YOU MAY BE TOLD TO MOVE A DOOR, INSTALL A
FOUNTAIN, OR PUT UP A MIRROR TO KEEP EVIL
FORCES AWAY.

FENG SHUI "WARS"
SOMETIMES ERUPT
WHEN NEIGHBORS
PUT UP MIRRORS TO
REFLECT EACH
OTHER'S BAD LUCK.

BE CAREFUL OF THE GESTURES YOU MAKE IN OTHER COUNTRIES. YOU COULD BE SAYING THINGS YOU DON'T MEAN!

SHAKING YOUR HEAD IN BULGARIA AND GREECE MEANS "YES." NODDING MEANS "NO."

DON'T GIVE SOMEONE A HIGH FIVE IN GREECE.
IT MEANS (ROUGHLY) "IN YOUR FACE."

AVOID POINTING THE SOLES OF YOUR FEET AT
PEOPLE IN SAUDI ARABIA, INDIA, AND SOUTHEAST
ASIA. IT'S INSULTING BECAUSE FEET TOUCH THE
GROUND, WHICH IS CONSIDERED FILTHY.

NEVER PAT SOMEONE ON THE HEAD IN THAILAND OR
OTHER BUDDHIST COUNTRIES. BUDDHISTS BELIEVE
THE HEAD IS SACRED.

IF EVERYONE SPOKE THE SAME LANGUAGE, MAYBE THEY'D FIND A WAY TO GET ALONG. THAT'S WHAT A POLISH EYE DOCTOR NAMED L. L. ZAMENHOF BELIEVED WHEN, IN 1887, HE INTRODUCED ESPERANTO, WHICH IS ESPERANTO FOR "ONE WHO HOPES." DR. ZAMENHOF BORROWED FROM SEVERAL EUROPEAN LANGUAGES AND SIMPLIFIED THE GRAMMAR SO IT WOULD BE EASY TO LEARN. FOR EXAMPLE, HE USED A SINGLE WORD, ESTAS, TO MEAN "IS," "AM," OR "ARE."

SOME ESPERANTO WORDS:

ESPERANTO NEVER CAUGHT ON, THOUGH, AND TODAY ENGLISH IS THE CLOSEST THERE IS TO A WORLD LANGUAGE. THERE ARE NOW HUNDREDS OF MILLIONS OF ENGLISH SPEAKERS, BUT ONLY A FEW MILLION ESPERANTO SPEAKERS.

IF YOU HAVE A SHORTWAVE RADIO, YOU CAN HEAR ESPERANTO PROGRAMS ON STATIONS FROM CHINA, CUBA, AND THE VATICAN. IT SOUNDS A BIT LIKE SPANISH OR ITALIAN.

IT'S A FACT!

THERE HAVE BEEN DOZENS OF OTHER "INTER-NATIONAL LANGUAGES," INCLUDING VOLAPÜK, INTERLINGUA, AND LOGLAN. PERHAPS THE WEIRDEST WAS SOLRESOL, MADE UP ENTIRELY OF MUSICAL NOTES. INTRODUCED BY A FRENCH MUSIC TEACHER IN 1827, IT HAD MORE THAN 11,000 WORDS THAT COULD BE SPOKEN, SUNG, OR PLAYED.

SNAKES HAVE BEEN PART OF RELIGIOUS CEREMONIES FOR THOUSANDS OF YEARS. IN SOME CULTURES THEY ARE SYMBOLS OF EVIL. IN OTHERS THEY REPRESENT WISDOM OR FERTILITY.

SNAKE RITUALS

THE HOPI PEOPLE BELIEVE THEY ARE DESCENDED FROM TWO SNAKE GODS, THE SNAKE HERO AND THE SNAKE MAID. IN AUGUST, CERTAIN TRIBE MEMBERS COLLECT BULL SNAKES AND RATTLESNAKES FROM THE DESERT; THEN THEY DANCE, HOLDING THE SNAKES IN THEIR TEETH. AFTER THE CEREMONY THEY RELEASE THE SNAKES TO ASK THE GODS FOR RAIN.

AS A TEST OF THEIR FAITH, MEMBERS OF SOME CHRISTIAN SECTS IN THE UNITED STATES HANDLE POISONOUS SNAKES WHILE THEY PRAY. MANY SNAKE HANDLERS HAVE BEEN BITTEN, AND A FEW HAVE DIED.

ON THE MALAYSIAN ISLAND OF PENANG THERE'S A FAMOUS SNAKE TEMPLE DEDICATED TO THE GOD CHOR SOO KONG. INSIDE, POISONOUS SNAKES SLITHER AROUND WHILE ATTENDANTS BURN INCENSE TO KEEP THEM DROWSY.

IT'S A FACT!

IN 1995 TWO CHINESE WOMEN SET A WORLD RECORD BY SPENDING 12 DAYS LOCKED UP WITH 888 SNAKES—INCLUDING 666 COBRAS AND 2 BOA CONSTRICTORS. THE SNAKES CRAWLED ALL OVER THEM AND SLEPT UNDER THEIR PILLOWS. ONE WOMAN WAS BITTEN BY A COBRA, BUT SHE SURVIVED BY TAKING HERBAL MEDICINE. IT WASN'T A RELIGIOUS RITUAL, BUT A PUBLICITY STUNT FOR A SNAKE THEME PARK IN SOUTHERN CHINA.

FOR YEARS, TALES HAVE BEEN TOLD OF HAITI'S ZOMBIES—THE "LIVING DEAD," WHO WALK IN A TRANCE AND DO SIMPLE MANUAL LABOR.

THERE REALLY HAVE BEEN ZOMBIES. THEIR ENEMIES WOULD GIVE THEM A SECRET VOODOO POTION THAT TEMPORARILY PARALYZED THEM, MAKING THEM SEEM DEAD.

THE POTION PROBABLY CONTAINED INTERNAL ORGANS FROM A POISONOUS PUFFER FISH.

ZOMBIES

AFTER THE FUNERAL, THE "ENEMIES" WOULD OPEN THEIR VICTIMS' GRAVES AND GIVE THEM OTHER DRUGS TO KEEP THEM IN A STUPOR.

HERE...DRINK THIS...

THEY'D LEAD THE ZOMBIES AWAY AND PUT THEM TO WORK AS SLAVES—SOMETIMES FOR YEARS. THE ZOMBIES' FAMILIES NEVER MISSED THEM, BECAUSE THEY WERE SUPPOSEDLY DEAD.

ARE THERE ZOMBIES IN HAITI NOW? PERHAPS, BUT NOBODY LIKES TO TALK ABOUT IT!

LOTS OF PEOPLE AROUND THE WORLD
EAT INSECTS—AND LIKE THEM! IT'S
REALLY NOT SO STRANGE, SINCE BUGS
ARE PLENTIFUL AND CONTAIN MORE
PROTEIN THAN MEAT DOES. SOME
BUGS TASTE LIKE NUTS, MEAT,
CHEESE, LETTUCE, OR SCRAMBLED
EGGS.

LOLLYPOPS WITH BUGS INSIDE WERE A
RECENT HIT WITH SWEDISH KIDS AND
ARE NOW SOLD IN THE UNITED STATES.
THE POPS COME IN TWO FLAVORS:
FRIED MEXICAN CACTUS WORM, AND
GRASSHOPPER.

LARGE FRIED ANTS ARE SOLD LIKE POPCORN AT COLOMBIAN MOVIE THEATERS.

MOPANIE WORMS—GIANT MOTH LARVAE FROM SOUTH AFRICA—ARE KNOWN AS "THE SNACK THAT CRAWLS." PEOPLE DRY THEM AND ADD THEM TO STEWS.

CHOCOLATE CHIRP COOKIES (WITH CRICKETS)!

WANT TO EAT BUGS? LOCAL INSECT CLUBS SOMETIMES HAVE TASTINGS AT WHICH YOU CAN SAMPLE INSECT TREATS. NOT ALL INSECTS ARE EDIBLE, THOUGH. SOME ARE POISONOUS OR CARRY DISEASES.

THERE'S NOTHING LIKE A LONG, UNPRONOUNCEABLE NAME TO KEEP THE TEACHER FROM CALLING ON YOU! HERE ARE SOME CREATIVE NAMES THAT PARENTS HAVE COME UP WITH FOR THEIR KIDS.

A GIRL NAMED RHOSHANDIATELLYNESHIAUNNEVESHENK KOYAANISQUATSIUTH WILLIAMS WAS BORN IN TEXAS IN 1984. WHEN SHE WAS THREE WEEKS OLD, HER FATHER CHANGED HER NAME SO IT HAD 1,063 LETTERS—ENOUGH TO FILL A 4-INCH-LONG NEWSPAPER COLUMN. ACCORDING TO *THE GUINNESS BOOK OF RECORDS*, THAT'S STILL THE WORLD'S LONGEST NAME.

A JUDGE IN SWEDEN RECENTLY FINED A COUPLE $600 FOR NAMING THEIR SON BRFXXCCXXMNPCCCCLLLMMNCKSSQLB-B111116. THEY NOW CALL HIM ALBIN.

IT'S A FACT!

ACCORDING TO OFFICIAL RECORDS, PEOPLE WITH THESE LAST NAMES HAVE LIVED IN THE UNITED STATES: PESKY, DULL, BORING, NASTY, CREEP, WORM, VIRUS, CHICKEN, TURKEY, FAILURE, UGLY, SNOT, MONEY, ELEVATORS, DIRTY, SHEEP, BATMAN, SPIDER, TEACUP, SQUIRREL, HAPPY, OVERALLS, AND THE NUMBERS ONE THROUGH TWELVE.

PLACES

HOTEL 30 FT.

HOTEL

IF YOU'VE EVER WANTED TO BECOME A KING OR QUEEN BUT WEREN'T BORN INTO ROYALTY, THERE'S A SIMPLE WAY TO DO IT: START YOUR OWN COUNTRY. THAT'S WHAT DOZENS OF PEOPLE HAVE DONE—AS A PROTEST, A MONEY-MAKING SCHEME, OR A JOKE. THE COUNTRIES MAY NOT BE RECOGNIZED NATIONS, BUT DON'T TELL THAT TO THEIR RULERS! LET'S VISIT A FEW OF THESE "MICRONATIONS."

KINGDOM OF NAVASSA ISLAND

IN 1976 AN AMERICAN NAMED DAVID P. BILLINGTON DECLARED HIMSELF KING OF THIS TINY, UNINHABITED CARIBBEAN ISLAND AND ANNOUNCED THAT HE WOULD USE IT TO DISTRIBUTE FREE BOOKS BY BALLOON. THE TROUBLE WAS, THE ISLAND HAD ALREADY BEEN CLAIMED BY BOTH THE U.S. AND HAITI. "KING DAVID" DID MAIL SOME ALMANACS TO NEIGHBORING ISLANDS, BUT HE NEVER GOT THE U.S. OR HAITI TO RECOGNIZE HIS SOVEREIGNTY. HE NOW LIVES IN CALIFORNIA, AND HIS ISLAND IS POPULATED ONLY BY BIRDS.

THE HUTT RIVER PROVINCE PRINCIPALITY

THIS 295-SQUARE-MILE NATION IN CENTRAL AUSTRALIA WAS FOUNDED IN 1970 BY A FARMING FAMILY THAT WAS UNHAPPY WITH AUSTRALIA'S WHEAT-GROWING POLICIES. THE PRINCIPALITY SUPPORTS ITSELF BY SELLING STAMPS, CURRENCY, PASSPORTS, AND NOBLE TITLES. IT HAS FORMALLY SECEDED FROM AUSTRALIA, BUT AUSTRALIA DOESN'T RECOGNIZE IT. ITS RULER IS PRINCE LEONARD GEORGE CASLEY.

THE CONCH REPUBLIC

IN 1982 THE U.S. BORDER PATROL SET UP A ROADBLOCK TO STOP SMUGGLERS AND ILLEGAL ALIENS ON THE NARROW ROAD THAT CONNECTS KEY WEST, FLORIDA, TO THE MAINLAND. LAW-ABIDING CITIZENS, INCLUDING KEY WEST'S MAYOR, WERE SO ANNOYED AT THE CONSTANT DELAYS THAT THEY STARTED THEIR OWN COUNTRY AS A PRANK. THEY NOW PUBLISH A MAGAZINE ON THE WORLDWIDE WEB AND SPONSOR AN "INDEPENDENCE" CELEBRA-TION EVERY APRIL. AS OF 1997, THE CONCH REPUBLIC'S SECRETARY GENERAL WAS THE HONORABLE SIR PETER ANDERSON.

WANT TO STAY SOMEWHERE REALLY DIFFERENT ON YOUR NEXT VACATION? TRY ONE OF THESE HOTELS.

JULES' UNDERSEA LODGE, IN FLORIDA'S KEY LARGO UNDERSEA PARK, IS A TWO-ROOM HOTEL THAT'S 30 FEET UNDERWATER! YOU CAN GET THERE ONLY BY DIVING. A ONE-NIGHT STAY COSTS $200 TO $300 PER PERSON, INCLUDING DINNER, BREAKFAST, AND AIR.

SPACE IS TIGHT IN JAPAN, SO SOMEONE INVENTED THE *KAPUSERU HOTERU,* OR "CAPSULE HOTEL." EACH CAPSULE SLEEPS ONE PERSON AND MEASURES 7 FEET LONG BY 4 FEET TALL AND 4 FEET WIDE. IT HAS A BUILT-IN MATTRESS, TV, RADIO, MIRROR, AND ALARM CLOCK. BATHROOMS ARE DOWN THE HALL. THE CAPSULES, USED BY BUSINESSMEN WHO HAVE STAYED OUT TOO LATE, ARE STACKED INSIDE BUILDINGS NEAR TRAIN STATIONS. THE $40 NIGHTLY RATE INCLUDES A TOOTHBRUSH AND PAJAMAS.

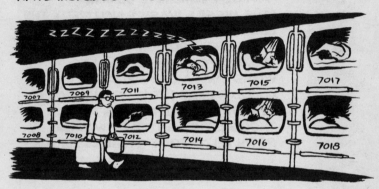

IN LAPLAND, CHECK OUT THE ICE HOTEL. IT'S IN THE TINY TOWN OF JUKKASJAERVI, 100 MILES NORTH OF THE ARCTIC CIRCLE. THE 10-ROOM HOTEL IS MADE ENTIRELY OF ICE AND SNOW. EVEN THE BEDS ARE BLOCKS OF ICE, COVERED WITH REINDEER SKINS SO THE GUESTS' BODY HEAT WON'T MELT THEM. STAYING THERE COSTS ABOUT $120 A NIGHT—BUT DON'T TRY VISITING IN SUMMER. THE ENTIRE HOTEL MELTS IN MAY AND HAS TO BE REBUILT EACH NOVEMBER.

KANSAS RESIDENTS ED AND DIANNA PEDEN NEVER WORRY ABOUT TORNADOES BLOWING DOWN THEIR HOUSE. THAT'S BECAUSE THEY LIVE UNDERGROUND IN A FORMER NUCLEAR MISSILE SILO. ED BOUGHT THE SURPLUS SILO FROM THE U.S. GOVERNMENT IN 1984, PAYING JUST $40,000 FOR THE 90-FOOT BY 40-FOOT CONCRETE BUNKER (THE MISSILE WASN'T INCLUDED). THE CEILINGS ARE 15 FEET HIGH, AND THE STEEL DOOR ON TOP WEIGHS 800,000 POUNDS—ENOUGH TO WITHSTAND A ONE-MEGATON NUCLEAR BLAST. THE PEDENS DON'T EVEN TRY TO BUDGE THIS DOOR, THOUGH. THEY ENTER BY WALKING DOWN A 120-FOOT STEEL-LINED TUBE.

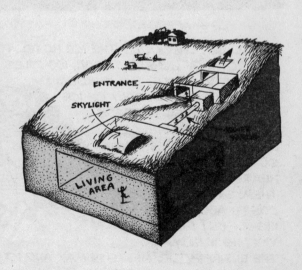

A FEW YEARS BACK, A REAL ESTATE MAGAZINE HELD A CONTEST TO FIND THE WEIRDEST HOMES IN THE UNITED STATES. THE WINNER WAS THIS REMODELED WATER TANK IN SEAL BEACH, CALIFORNIA. IT HAS THREE BEDROOMS AND WRAPAROUND VIEWS OF THE OCEAN. IT STANDS 87 FEET ABOVE THE BEACH.

THIS UFO-SHAPED HOUSE NEAR CHATTANOOGA, TENNESSEE, WAS THE RUNNER-UP. IT HAS THREE BEDROOMS AND TWO BATHS.

GIANT SCALE MODELS

NEXT TIME YOU'RE TRAVELING AROUND THE U.S., CHECK OUT THESE KING-SIZE MINIATURE ATTRACTIONS.

THE WORLD'S LARGEST SCALE MODEL OF OUR SOLAR SYSTEM IS LOCATED IN AND AROUND PEORIA, ILLINOIS. IT WAS BUILT TO GIVE PEOPLE AN IDEA OF THE HUGE DISTANCES BETWEEN PLANETS. THE SUN IS PAINTED ON THE PLANETARIUM DOME OF PEORIA'S LAKEVIEW MUSEUM OF ARTS AND SCIENCES. PLUTO IS A ONE-INCH BALL 40 MILES AWAY.

42 FEET = 1 MILLION MILES

BEFORE THE AGE OF COMPUTER SIMULATION, PLANNERS HAD TO BUILD SCALE MODELS TO TEST THEIR THEORIES AND DESIGNS.

IN SAUSALITO, CALIFORNIA, THERE'S A WORKING MODEL OF SAN FRANCISCO BAY THAT'S AS BIG AS TWO FOOTBALL FIELDS. THE U.S. ARMY CORPS OF ENGINEERS BUILT IT IN 1957 TO TEST WHERE OIL SPILLS WOULD GO AND HOW NEW STRUCTURES WOULD AFFECT THE FLOW OF TIDES. ITS AUTOMATED PUMPS CHANGE THE TIDE EVERY 3.7 MINUTES— A HUNDRED TIMES FASTER THAN NORMAL.

SAN FRANCISCO BAY MODEL

GOLDEN GATE BR.

ALCATRAZ

1 FOOT = 1000 FT.

SAN FRANCISCO

BAY BRIDGE

A COMPLETE SCALE MODEL OF NEW YORK CITY, INCLUDING EVERY BUILDING, BRIDGE, AND STREET, IS ON DISPLAY AT THE QUEENS MUSEUM IN FLUSHING, NEW YORK. BIGGER THAN THREE TENNIS COURTS, IT WAS ORIGINALLY PART OF THE 1964-65 NEW YORK WORLD'S FAIR, WHERE IT WAS BILLED AS THE WORLD'S LARGEST SCALE MODEL. IN 1994 CURATORS UPDATED IT BY ADDING 95,000 NEW BUILDINGS, BRINGING THE TOTAL TO 895,000.

1 INCH = 100 FEET
EMPIRE STATE BUILDING = 15 INCHES

THERE HAVE BEEN NUMEROUS MYTHS ABOUT SUBTERRANEAN CITIES, BUT HERE ARE SOME THAT HAVE ACTUALLY EXISTED.

IN THE REGION CALLED CAPPADOCIA, NOW PART OF TURKEY, THERE ARE UNDERGROUND CITIES DATING BACK MORE THAN 2,000 YEARS! ANCIENT HITTITES PROBABLY CARVED THESE CITIES INTO THE SOFT ROCK TO ESCAPE FREQUENT WARFARE. LATER, EARLY CHRISTIANS HID THERE FROM PERSECUTORS.

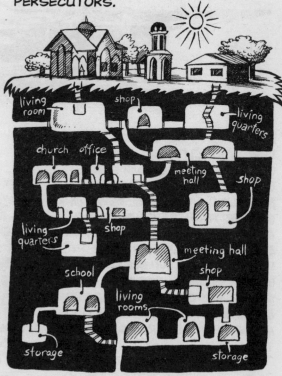

KAYMAKLI

THE CITY OF KAYMAKLI GOES DOWN 8 LEVELS AND WAS ONCE HOME TO 15,000 PEOPLE. ITS UNDER-GROUND APARTMENTS, CHURCHES, AND MEETING ROOMS HAD THEIR OWN SYSTEM OF AIR SHAFTS AND WATER WELLS. NEARBY DERINKUYU IS EVEN BIGGER, WITH AT LEAST 20 LEVELS THAT MAY HAVE HAD 20,000 INHABITANTS.

ARCHAEOLOGISTS THINK THERE MAY BE AS MANY AS 30 MORE CITIES UNDER CAPPADOCIA, PERHAPS LINKED BY UNDERGROUND PASSAGES.

TO ESCAPE ITS FREEZING WINTERS, MONTREAL, CANADA, HAS BUILT A HUGE NETWORK OF UNDERGROUND CORRIDORS THAT CONNECT MANY PARTS OF TOWN. IT'S CALLED THE VILLE SOUTERRAINE, OR UNDERGROUND CITY. ALONG ITS 18 MILES OF PASSAGEWAYS YOU CAN WALK TO 1,700 BUSINESSES, 1,600 STORES, 1,615 DWELLINGS, 200 RESTAURANTS, 45 BANKS, 34 THEATERS, 8 HOTELS, A BRANCH LIBRARY, 2 UNIVERSITIES, 2 EXHIBITION HALLS, AND BUS, TRAIN, AND SUBWAY STATIONS GOING DOWN 5 LEVELS.

PARIS, TOKYO, NEW YORK, AND ATLANTA ALSO HAVE UNDERGROUND COMPLEXES, SOME OF THEM QUITE LARGE.

THE NIGHTS ARE QUIET IN COLMA, CALIFORNIA—WHICH IS JUST THE WAY MOST OF THE PEOPLE THERE LIKE IT. THAT'S BECAUSE THEY'RE DEAD. FOR EVERY LIVING RESIDENT, COLMA HAS 1,200 DEAD ONES, WHO ARE BURIED IN 17 CEMETERIES BLANKETING THE TOWN'S 2.2 SQUARE MILES.

MOST OF COLMA'S 1.5 MILLION DECEASED WERE MOVED THERE AFTER 1898, WHEN NEIGHBORING SAN FRANCISCO MADE IT ILLEGAL TO BURY PEOPLE WITHIN CITY LIMITS.

COLMA'S DEAD CELEBRITIES INCLUDE GUNFIGHTER WYATT EARP, BLUE JEANS TYCOON LEVI STRAUSS, AND TINA TURNER'S DOG.

IF YOU'RE ALIVE, THERE ISN'T MUCH TO DO IN COLMA EXCEPT VISIT THE GRAVES OR SHOP AT LOCAL MALLS. AND IF YOU'RE DEAD, YOU MIGHT AS WELL JUST LIE AROUND!

TECHNOLOGY

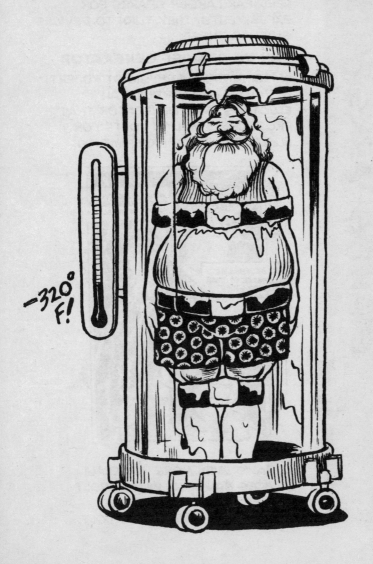

-320°
F!

WHEN YOU GET A SHOCK AFTER WALKING ACROSS A CARPET, THAT'S BECAUSE OF STATIC ELECTRICITY. THE ENERGY YOU RELEASE THAT WAY CAN EXCEED 15,000 VOLTS. WHEN SCIENTISTS NEED FAR LARGER SPARKS FOR EXPERIMENTS, THEY TURN TO DEVICES SUCH AS THESE.

VAN DE GRAAFF GENERATOR

IN 1931 AMERICAN PHYSICIST ROBERT J. VAN DE GRAAFF BUILT AN ELECTROSTATIC GENERATOR THAT PRODUCED 5 MILLION VOLTS FOR NUCLEAR PHYSICS EXPERIMENTS.

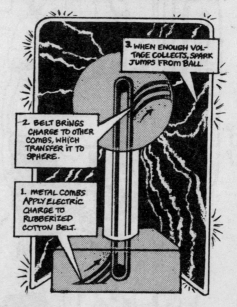

3. WHEN ENOUGH VOLTAGE COLLECTS, SPARK JUMPS FROM BALL.

2. BELT BRINGS CHARGE TO OTHER COMBS, WHICH TRANSFER IT TO SPHERE.

1. METAL COMBS APPLY ELECTRIC CHARGE TO RUBBERIZED COTTON BELT.

TODAY'S EVEN MORE POWERFUL DEVICES CAN MAKE BILLION-VOLT SPARKS—WITH THE ZAPPING POTENTIAL OF A LIGHTNING BOLT.

GIANT SPARKS

TESLA COIL

NIKOLA TESLA MADE HISTORY IN 1888 BY INVENTING THE ALTERNATING-CURRENT GENERATOR, WHICH MADE IT ECONOMICAL TO SEND ELECTRIC POWER OVER LONG DISTANCES. NEXT HE INVENTED THE TESLA COIL, WHICH EVENTUALLY MADE RADIO TRANSMISSION POSSIBLE. THEN HE DECIDED TO THINK *REALLY* BIG. INSPIRED BY LIGHTNING, HE BUILT A GIANT COIL TO SEND ELECTRIC POWER THROUGH THE AIR—*WITHOUT WIRES!*

ALTHOUGH MILLIONS OF VOLTS WERE INVOLVED, THE CURRENT WAS SMALL AND NOT DANGEROUS. TO PROVE IT, TESLA WOULD HOOK HIMSELF UP TO A COIL SO THAT SPARKS FLEW FROM HIS FINGERS AND HAIR. TESLA'S INVENTION WASN'T SUCCESSFUL, BUT IT WAS DRAMATIC.

SOME CRYSTALS CAN GENERATE ELECTRICITY WHEN YOU PRESS ON THEM—AN EFFECT KNOWN AS "PIEZOELECTRICITY." (PIEZO, PRONOUNCED "PEA-AY-ZO," COMES FROM THE GREEK WORD FOR "PRESS.") THEIR ATOMS ARE ARRANGED IN A WAY THAT MAKES THEM SHED ELECTRONS WHEN THE ATOMS ARE UNDER PRESSURE. THIS CAUSES A CURRENT TO FLOW.

A U.S. COMPANY HAS INVENTED A PIEZOELECTRIC DEVICE THAT USES OCEAN WAVES TO GENERATE ELECTRICITY! SHEETS OF PLASTIC EMBEDDED WITH PIEZOELECTRIC CRYSTALS ARE STRETCHED BETWEEN AN ANCHOR AND A FLOAT. WAVES BEND THE PLASTIC, PRODUCING ELECTRIC CURRENT THAT CAN BE SENT TO SHORE BY CABLE. THE COMPANY THINKS THAT ONE DAY, OFFSHORE "FARMS" OF THESE DEVICES COULD GENERATE ELECTRICITY MORE CHEAPLY THAN GAS, OIL, OR COAL.

YOU CAN OBSERVE ONE KIND OF PIEZOELECTRICITY BY CHOMPING ON A WINT-O-GREEN LIFE SAVER. (PINK NECCO WAFERS ALSO WORK.) GO IN A DARK ROOM AND HOLD A MIRROR TO YOUR MOUTH AS YOU CRUNCH THE CANDY. IF ALL GOES WELL, YOU SHOULD SEE A BRIEF FLASH OF LIGHT!

WHY? CRUSHING SUGAR CRYSTALS PRODUCES A TINY, INVISIBLE SPARK, WHICH MAKES THE CANDY'S WINTERGREEN FLAVORING FLUORESCE. THIS LIGHT IS CALLED *TRIBOLUMINESCENCE* (**TRIBE-OH-LOOM-IN-ESS-ENCE**), FROM THE GREEK WORD FOR "RUB."

IF YOU EVER NEED TO SPY ON SOMEONE, IT PAYS TO HAVE THE RIGHT EQUIPMENT. THESE HANDY GADGETS ARE AVAILABLE FROM "SPY STORES" IN A FEW U.S. CITIES. IF YOU'RE A GOOD ENOUGH SPY, YOU SHOULD HAVE NO TROUBLE FINDING THEM.

SPY GEAR

MINI-CAM HIDDEN IN CAP

PINHOLE CAMERA IN GLASSES FRAME

WHENEVER YOU PEER THROUGH THESE $7,000 EYEGLASSES, YOU ARE ALSO VIDEOTAPING—THANKS TO A PINHOLE CAMERA IN THE FRAME THAT SENDS TV PICTURES TO A HIDDEN VCR (NOT INCLUDED). OR YOU CAN HIDE THIS $800 MATCHBOX-SIZE MINI-CAM IN YOUR HAT.

FOR DANGEROUS MISSIONS THAT ARE ALSO DAMP, TAKE ALONG THIS BULLETPROOF UMBRELLA MADE OF KEVLAR.

PEOPLE WHO PRY INSIDE THIS HIGH-SECURITY BRIEFCASE WILL BE SHOCKED BY WHAT THEY FIND—50,000 VOLTS!

DOCTORS OFTEN FREEZE SKIN AND BLOOD TO PRESERVE THEM FOR MEDICAL EMERGENCIES. BUT THEY CAN'T YET FREEZE WHOLE ORGANS, BECAUSE ICE CRYSTALS WOULD DAMAGE THEM.

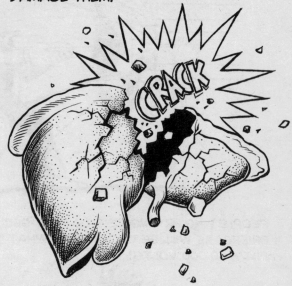

NEVERTHELESS, MORE THAN 65 PEOPLE HAVE HAD THEIR BODIES—OR JUST THEIR HEADS—FROZEN AFTER DEATH IN THE HOPE THAT IT WILL ONE DAY BE POSSIBLE TO REVIVE THEM. (PRESUMABLY, THEIR HEADS WILL BE ATTACHED TO NEW BODIES.)

THE CORPSES ARE CHILLED TO THE TEMPERATURE OF LIQUID NITROGEN— MINUS 320 DEGREES FAHRENHEIT— AND STORED INSIDE GIANT THERMOS BOTTLES. THIS PRACTICE IS CALLED CRYONICS (CRY-ON-ICKS).

EVEN IF THE POWER GOES OUT, THE THERMOSES CAN KEEP PEOPLE FROZEN FOR CENTURIES IF THEIR LIQUID NITROGEN COOLANT IS REPLACED OCCASIONALLY.

−320° F!

WILL CRYONICS WORK? MAYBE; MAYBE NOT. IT DEPENDS ON WHETHER FUTURE PEOPLE WILL BE ABLE TO REVIVE THE FROZEN DEAD—AND CURE WHAT KILLED THEM. IT ALSO DEPENDS ON WHETHER THEY WILL EVEN WANT TO.

43

HIGH-TECH TOILETS

THE MODERN TOILET HAS BEEN AROUND FOR MORE THAN A CENTURY, SO IT'S HIGH TIME FOR A FEW IMPROVEMENTS. HERE ARE EXAMPLES FROM THE LATEST FLUSH OF TOILET TECHNOLOGY.

THIS IS THE WEIRDEST ATM I'VE EVER SEEN!

AUTOMATED TOILETS ARE COMMON ON THE STREETS OF EUROPE, AND A FEW HAVE BEEN INTRODUCED IN THE U.S. INSERTING A COIN OPENS THE DOOR THAT LETS YOU IN. AFTER YOU LEAVE, CHEMICALS ARE SPRAYED OVER THE FLOOR, SINK, AND TOILET BOWL TO DISINFECT THEM FOR THE NEXT PERSON.

THE TOILET ON NASA'S SPACE SHUTTLE HAS A SEAT BELT, HAND HOLDS, AND FOOT RESTRAINTS TO KEEP ASTRONAUTS FROM FLOATING IN ZERO GRAVITY. THERE'S EVEN A WINDOW SO THEY CAN GAZE INTO SPACE WHILE DOING THEIR BUSINESS. JETS OF AIR FLUSH WASTE INTO A SEPARATE CONTAINER. SOLID WASTE IS BROUGHT HOME, BUT LIQUID WASTE IS EJECTED INTO SPACE (SEE "SPACE JUNK," PAGE 88).

JAPAN HAS SOME OF THE WORLD'S MOST ADVANCED TOILETS. A MODEL CALLED THE WASHLET, POPULAR IN HOMES, SPRAYS WATER ON YOUR BEHIND AND THEN BLOW-DRIES IT. IT HAS A HEATED SEAT AND AN ODOR FILTER THAT IS ACTIVATED WHEN YOU SIT DOWN. NEWER KINDS CAN ALSO MEASURE YOUR BLOOD PRESSURE AND CHECK YOUR PULSE.

OVER THE YEARS, CLOCKMAKERS HAVE COME UP WITH INGENIOUS WAYS OF MAKING CLOCKS RUN. HERE ARE SOME EXAMPLES.

INVENTED BY SWISS ENGINEER JEAN-LEON REUTTER IN 1927, THE ATMOS CLOCK IS POWERED BY CHANGES IN TEMPERATURE AND NEVER NEEDS BATTERIES OR WINDING. A SEALED CHAMBER INSIDE THE CLOCK CONTAINS A GAS THAT MAKES THE CHAMBER EXPAND WHEN THE TEMPERATURE GOES UP—AND CONTRACT WHEN IT GOES DOWN. THIS ACCORDION MOTION WINDS A MAINSPRING THAT DRIVES THE GEARS AND HANDS. AT ROOM TEMPERATURE, A CHANGE OF JUST ONE DEGREE FAHRENHEIT CAN RUN THE CLOCK FOR TWO DAYS.

YOU MIGHT TAKE A LICKIN' AND KEEP ON TICKIN,' BUT I NEVER NEED BATTERIES OR WINDING!

ATMOS

AN ELECTRIC CLOCK INVENTED BY SCOTTISH
CLOCKMAKER ALEXANDER BAIN IN THE MID-1800S
USED THE EARTH AS A BATTERY! TWO METAL
ELECTRODES—ONE ZINC, ONE COPPER—WERE STUCK
INTO DAMP SOIL NOT FAR APART. THE METALS'
DIFFERING ELECTRICAL PROPERTIES GENERATED
ABOUT ONE VOLT OF ELECTRICITY, USING THE SAME
PRINCIPLE AS A DRY-CELL BATTERY.

A MODERN VARIATION ON THE EARTH CLOCK IS
POWERED BY TWO LEMONS. ACID IN THE LEMONS
ENABLES A SMALL CURRENT TO FLOW BETWEEN THE
ZINC AND COPPER ELECTRODES. THE BATTERY LASTS
FOR SEVERAL WEEKS. (MANY OTHER FRUITS OR
VEGETABLES ALSO WORK.)

YOU WON'T FIND THESE VEHICLES AT YOUR LOCAL CAR DEALERSHIP, BUT THEY ACTUALLY EXIST!

THE AQUASTRADA DELTA AMPHIBIOUS CAR HAS WHEELS THAT RETRACT SO YOU CAN USE IT AS A BOAT. IT CAN GO 100 MILES PER HOUR ON LAND AND 45 MPH IN THE WATER. DESIGNED BY A CALIFORNIA COMPANY, IT SELLS FOR AROUND $30,000.

A WALKING MOTORCYCLE WAS RECENTLY DEMONSTRATED AT JAPAN'S TOYOTA IDEA OLYMPICS, A YEARLY SHOWCASE FOR THE TOYOTA ENGINEERS' WILDEST IDEAS.

THIS 72-FOOT S-T-R-E-T-C-H LIMOUSINE WAS BUILT FOR SHEIK HAMAD BIN HANDAN AL-NAHYAN IN 1996, AT A COST OF $1.8 MILLION. IT SEATS 38 PEOPLE AND BENDS IN THE MIDDLE SO IT CAN TURN CORNERS.

DRIVER-WE MISSED OUR TURN-AGAIN!

IT'S A FACT!
JAPANESE ENGINEERS RECENTLY CREATED A WORKING ELECTRIC CAR NO BIGGER THAN A MATCH HEAD. MODELED AFTER A 1936 TOYOTA SEDAN, THE "MICRO-CAR" WAS BUILT TO TEST MANUFACTURING TECHNIQUES FOR TINY MACHINES OF THE FUTURE. IT COST MORE TO MAKE THAN A FULL-SIZE CAR.

PERFECTED IN THE 1950S, THIS STRANGE CRAFT FLOATS A FEW FEET OFF THE GROUND ON A CUSHION OF AIR. POWERFUL FANS LIFT IT UP AND PUSH IT FORWARD.

LARGE HOVERCRAFT HAVE FERRIED PEOPLE ACROSS THE ENGLISH CHANNEL FOR NEARLY 30 YEARS. THESE FERRIES GO 70 MILES AN HOUR—MUCH FASTER THAN A BOAT. SOME CARRY MORE THAN 400 PASSENGERS AND 60 CARS.

OTHER HOVERCRAFT, DESIGNED FOR LAND TRAVEL, CAN EITHER HOVER OR ROLL.

AN AMAZING NEW KIND OF HOVERCRAFT CAN GO 500
MILES AN HOUR—AS FAST AS A COMMERCIAL JET!
CALLED A WINGSHIP OR *EKRANOPLAN* (RUSSIAN FOR
"SCREEN PLANE"), IT WAS DEVELOPED BY SOVIET
ENGINEERS DURING THE COLD WAR. IT FLIES 15 TO 30
FEET ABOVE WATER OR FLAT LAND. STAYING THAT
LOW COMPRESSES AIR BENEATH THE CRAFT AND
HELPS IT FLY. ENGINEERS CALL THIS THE "GROUND
EFFECT."

A PROPOSED U.S. MODEL IS MORE THAN TWICE AS
LONG AS A BOEING 747. IT COULD ONE DAY CARRY
3,000 PASSENGERS ACROSS THE SEAS LIKE A FLYING
OCEAN LINER.

BURIED UNDER NEW YORK CITY ARE
DOZENS OF ABANDONED TRAIN
TUNNELS, SOME OF WHICH HAVE NOT
BEEN USED—OR EVEN SEEN—FOR
DECADES. BY FAR THE WEIRDEST IS
THE BLOCK-LONG BEACH PNEUMATIC
TRANSIT LINE IN LOWER MANHATTAN.
BUILT BY PUBLISHER-INVENTOR ALFRED
ELY BEACH IN 1870, THIS EXPERIMENTAL
AIR-DRIVEN TRAIN WAS NEW YORK'S
FIRST SUBWAY.

ITS SINGLE CAR WAS BLOWN
THROUGH THE TUNNEL BY A GIANT
STEAM-POWERED FAN. WHEN THE CAR
REACHED THE END OF THE LINE, THE
FAN CHANGED DIRECTION AND SUCKED
IT BACK AGAIN.

BUT BEACH'S IDEA DIDN'T CATCH ON.
HE CLOSED THE LINE AFTER ONLY A
FEW YEARS AND IT WAS SOON
FORGOTTEN. IN 1912, MODERN SUBWAY
BUILDERS WERE ASTONISHED TO
FIND THE BEACH LINE STILL INTACT,
COMPLETE WITH PNEUMATIC CAR!

BURIED TRAIN

ANIMALS & PLANTS

THE ONLY ACROBATICS MOST FLEAS DO IS TO JUMP FROM ONE WARM-BLOODED ANIMAL TO ANOTHER.

HOWEVER, IN DECADES PAST, FLEA CIRCUSES WERE FAMILIAR ATTRACTIONS AT AMUSEMENT PARKS AND COUNTRY FAIRS. NOW THERE ARE ONLY A FEW LEFT.

IN SAN FRANCISCO, AN ARTIST NAMED MARIA FERNANDA CARDOSO HAS TRAINED FLEAS TO PERFORM A VARIETY OF CIRCUS ACTS. AT HER CARDOSO FLEA CIRCUS, FLEA CLOWNS, TIGHTROPE WALKERS, WEIGHT LIFTERS, AND GLADIATORS IN TINY COSTUMES ENTERTAIN PEOPLE WITH MINUSCULE PROPS. WEARING MAGNIFYING GOGGLES AND A SILVERY CAPE, CARDOSO CRACKS A MINIATURE WHIP AS SHE URGES THE BLOOD-SUCKING INSECTS TO PERFORM.

TO TRAIN THE FLEAS, CARDOSO HARNESSES THEM
WITH TINY THREADS UNTIL THEY LEARN TO WALK ON
TWO LEGS. EACH FLEA LEARNS ONLY ONE TRICK.

FOR A SWORD FIGHT, SHE ATTACHES TINY SWORDS
TO THE FLEAS' FRONT LEGS. THEY APPEAR TO
"FIGHT" AS THEY TRY TO THROW THE SWORDS AWAY.

TO PULL A WAGON, THE FLEA IS HARNESSED IN
PLACE. A FLEA CAN PULL 2.5 OUNCES—160,000 TIMES
ITS OWN WEIGHT. TO BE THAT STRONG, A 150-POUND
HUMAN WOULD HAVE TO PULL 24 MILLION POUNDS.

THE FLEAS LIVE FOR ABOUT 2 MONTHS AND FEED ON
BLOOD FROM CARDOSO'S OWN ARM.

GLOWING PLANTS

BIOLOGISTS HAVE "BORROWED" GENES FROM GLOWING JELLYFISH, FIREFLIES, AND LUMINOUS BACTERIA TO CREATE PLANTS THAT GLOW IN THE DARK! THE GLOWING PLANTS AREN'T JUST FOR FUN—THEY'RE USED TO TEST THEORIES ABOUT PLANT BIOLOGY.

A RESEARCHER IN SCOTLAND USED JELLYFISH GENES TO CREATE PLANTS THAT GLOW WHEN UNDER STRESS. THEY EMIT LIGHT WHEN THEY ARE JABBED WITH A NEEDLE, DRIBBLED WITH ICE WATER, OR JUST TOUCHED. THE LIGHT IS TOO DIM TO SEE, BUT IT CAN BE PICKED UP BY A SENSITIVE CAMERA.

HAHA! HEE HEE!

A CALIFORNIA PROFESSOR IS WORKING ON GLOW-IN-THE-DARK CHRISTMAS TREES, USING GENES FROM GLOWING BACTERIA. HIS GENETICALLY ALTERED TREES DON'T GLOW BRIGHTLY YET, BUT HE HOPES THAT WITH MORE RESEARCH THEY WILL.

HE IS ALSO TRYING TO DEVELOP GLOWING BUSHES THAT COULD BE PLANTED ALONG HIGHWAYS TO MAKE DRIVING SAFER AT NIGHT.

NOW I HAVE TO WEAR SUNGLASSES AT NIGHT!

MUSHROOMS ARE THE "FRUITS" OF FUNGUS ORGANISMS—AND THEY'RE SOME OF THE WEIRDEST THINGS ALIVE.

GIANT PUFFBALLS GROW SO BIG THAT PEOPLE SOMETIMES MISTAKE THEM FOR GRAZING SHEEP.

CALVATIA GIGANTEA

A FEW HOURS AFTER THEY COME UP, INKY CAP MUSHROOMS BEGIN TO DISSOLVE INTO A BLACK FLUID YOU CAN WRITE WITH.

COPRINUS ATRAMENTARIUS

WOOD THAT HAS HONEY MUSHROOMS GROWING FROM
IT GLOWS IN THE DARK. PIECES OF THE WOOD, KNOWN
AS FOX FIRE, WERE ONCE USED TO MARK PATHS AT
NIGHT.

ARMILLARIA MELLEA

WILD MUSHROOMS MAY LOOK GOOD TO EAT—BUT
DON'T TRY THEM! SOME KINDS ARE DEADLY
POISONOUS.

IT'S A FACT!
BIOLOGISTS RECENTLY DISCOVERED THAT FUNGI
ARE MORE CLOSELY RELATED TO PEOPLE THAN
TO PLANTS!

IT SOUNDS INCREDIBLE, BUT SOME LIVING THINGS CAN WAIT HUNDREDS, THOUSANDS, OR MAYBE EVEN MILLIONS OF YEARS BEFORE SPRINGING TO LIFE.

SCIENTISTS RECENTLY ANNOUNCED THAT THEY HAD BROUGHT 25- TO 40-MILLION-YEAR-OLD BACTERIA BACK TO LIFE. THE BACTERIA WERE IN THE FORM OF SPORES—A RESTING STAGE WITH A THICK OUTER SHELL—THAT THE SCIENTISTS CLAIMED HAD BEEN PRESERVED INSIDE AN EXTINCT BEE IN A PIECE OF AMBER. IF OTHER RESEARCH BACKS UP THIS ASTOUNDING CLAIM, IT COULD MEAN THAT LIFE FORMS HALF AS OLD AS *TYRANNOSAURUS REX* ARE LIVING AGAIN.

BACK TO LIFE!

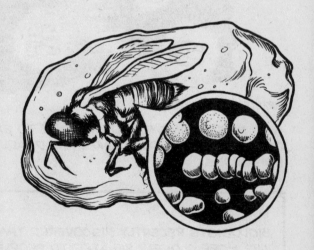

A 1,288-YEAR-OLD LOTUS SEED WAS SPROUTED IN 1983 BY AN AMERICAN BOTANIST. IT CAME FROM A DRY LAKE BED IN CHINA AND WAS THOUGHT TO BE THE OLDEST SEED EVER TO GERMINATE. SCIENTISTS THINK THE SEED STAYED ALIVE SO LONG BECAUSE ITS THICK SHELL KEPT OUT AIR AND WATER. IT MAY ALSO HAVE CONTAINED A CHEMICAL THAT WAS ABLE TO REPAIR THE DAMAGE CAUSED BY AGING.

BIOLOGISTS RECENTLY HATCHED 330-YEAR-OLD EGGS FROM TINY CRUSTACEANS IN RHODE ISLAND. THE EGGS WERE LAID IN THE BOTTOM OF A POND ABOUT 27 YEARS AFTER THE COLONY WAS FOUNDED.

330 YEARS AGO.....

I WONDER IF WE'LL LIVE TO SEE THEM GROW UP?

THESE GIANTS OF THE DEEP MAY LOOK SCARY, BUT THEY AREN'T INTERESTED IN EATING YOU. THEY PREFER SMALL ANIMALS AND PLANTS.

PACIFIC GIANT OCTOPUS (OCTOPUS DOFLEINI)

THE BIGGEST-EVER OCTOPUS MEASURED 31 FEET FROM TENTACLE TO TENTACLE. HOWEVER, THIS SHY, INTELLIGENT RELATIVE OF THE SQUID WOULD RATHER HIDE THAN ATTACK.

IT'S A FACT!

A GIANT, 26-FOOT-LONG SQUID WEIGHING ONE TON WAS CAUGHT NEAR NEW ZEALAND IN 1996. EXPERTS THINK EVEN BIGGER SQUIDS—UP TO 60 FEET LONG— MAY LIVE DEEP IN THE OCEANS.

WHALE SHARK (*RHINCODON TYPUS*)

THE WORLD'S BIGGEST KNOWN FISH GROWS UP TO
60 FEET LONG. (BLUE WHALES CAN GROW TO 100
FEET, BUT THEY'RE MAMMALS.) THE WHALE SHARK
HAS THOUSANDS OF POINTY TEETH. ODDLY, IT
DOESN'T CHEW FOOD WITH THEM—
IT EATS BY STRAINING TINY
PLANKTON THROUGH BONY
STRUCTURES NEAR
ITS GILLS.

GIANT CLAM (*TRIDACNA GIGAS*)

THIS SOUTH PACIFIC NATIVE GROWS TO BE ALMOST
5 FEET LONG AND WEIGHS OVER 500 POUNDS. BUT
NO NEED TO FEAR; IT WON'T CLAMP DOWN ON YOU—
IT EATS ONLY ALGAE.

SAY "AH".

CALLING SOMEONE A "BIRD BRAIN"
MEANS YOU THINK THEY ARE STUPID.
MAYBE IT'S TIME TO RETHINK THAT
INSULT!

AT THE UNIVERSITY OF ARIZONA, AN
AFRICAN GRAY PARROT NAMED ALEX
HAS LEARNED THE NAMES OF DOZENS
OF SHAPES, COLORS, MATERIALS, AND
SMALL OBJECTS. HIS TRAINER, DR.
IRENE PEPPERBERG, HAS PROVEN THAT
ALEX ISN'T JUST MEMORIZING—HE'S
THINKING. ALEX CAN COUNT UP TO 6
OBJECTS AND TELL IF THEY ARE THE
SAME OR DIFFERENT. DR. PEPPERBERG
THINKS THIS COULD MEAN THAT
PARROTS ARE AS SMART AS
CHIMPANZEES OR DOLPHINS.

BRAINY BIRDS

CROWS IN THE NEW CALEDONIA RAIN FOREST HAVE
RECENTLY BEEN OBSERVED MAKING TOOLS! A
BIOLOGIST WATCHED THEM PULL THE LEAVES OFF
TWIGS AND SHORTEN THEM TO CREATE HOOKS FOR
PULLING INSECTS OUT OF CREVICES. THE CROWS
ALSO TRIMMED LEAVES INTO POINTED SHAPES FOR
CUTTING. THEY USED THE SAME TOOLS FOR
DIFFERENT PURPOSES—SOMETHING THAT ONLY
HUMANS WERE THOUGHT TO DO.

EACH FALL, NUTCRACKERS BURY NUTS IN THE GROUND
SO THEY'LL HAVE FOOD DURING THE WINTER.
RESEARCHERS HAVE WATCHED INDIVIDUAL BIRDS
BURY MORE THAN 1,000 STASHES OF NUTS—AND
REMEMBER WHERE THEY ALL ARE.

THESE BARNYARD ODDITIES HAVE BEEN BRED OVER MANY YEARS FOR THEIR UNUSUAL TRAITS. SINCE MOST ARE MORE WEIRD THAN USEFUL, THEY ARE KEPT MAINLY AS PETS.

WHEN THE FAINTING GOAT IS SURPRISED OR FRIGHTENED, IT BECOMES TEMPORARILY PARALYZED AND FALLS OVER. THIS FREAK INHERITED CONDITION WAS DISCOVERED IN THE 1880S IN TENNESSEE, WHERE FARMERS RAISED THE GOATS TO PROTECT FLOCKS OF SHEEP. IF COYOTES ATTACKED, THE GOATS WOULD "FAINT" AND BE EATEN—WHILE THE SHEEP RAN AWAY UNHARMED.

THE JAPANESE LONG-TAILED
ROOSTER HAS TAIL FEATHERS THAT
KEEP GROWING UNTIL THEY ARE UP TO
25 FEET LONG. FIRST BRED ABOUT 300
YEARS AGO BY CROSSING NORMAL
CHICKENS WITH PHEASANTS, THESE
EXOTIC BIRDS ARE KEPT ON HIGH
PERCHES SO THEIR FEATHERS WON'T
BREAK OFF.

THE MINIATURE HORSE IS JUST HALF AS
TALL AS A STANDARD HORSE—LESS
THAN 34 INCHES AT THE BASE OF ITS
MANE. IT WAS DEVELOPED IN EUROPE BY
BREEDING SMALLER AND SMALLER
NORMAL HORSES TOGETHER FOR 200
YEARS. THE HORSES CAN BE RIDDEN BY
YOUNG CHILDREN, OR THEY CAN PULL
LITTLE WAGONS.

IT'S A FACT!
THESE RARE BREEDS ARE NATURALLY SMALL.
THEY HAVE BECOME POPULAR AS PETS.
• DEXTER CATTLE—ABOUT 4 FEET TALL
• MINIATURE DONKEY—ABOUT 3 FEET
• POTBELLIED PIG—15 INCHES
• OLDE ENGLISH BABY DOLL SOUTHDOWN SHEEP—
  UNDER 2 FEET

SOME CATS AND DOGS HAVE LITTLE OR NO HAIR, THANKS TO A MUTATION IN A GENE THAT CONTROLS HAIRINESS. THESE ANIMALS MAKE LOVING PETS, BUT THEY CHILL EASILY. THEY ALSO NEED TO WEAR SUNSCREEN IF THEY GO OUTSIDE.

THE *XOLOITZCUINTLI* (SHO-LO-EATS-**QUEENT**-LEE), OR MEXICAN HAIRLESS DOG, DATES BACK TO THE ANCIENT AZTECS. IT HAS ONLY TRACES OF HAIR ON ITS HEAD, FEET, AND TAIL.

SPHYNX CATS ARE COVERED WITH FINE DOWN, WHICH YOU CAN HARDLY SEE OR FEEL. AS THEY AGE, EVEN THIS FALLS OFF AND THEIR BODIES WRINKLE. THE FIRST SPHYNX APPEARED IN A CANADIAN LITTER IN 1966.

THERE ARE ICEBERGS FLOATING IN THE OCEANS THAT ARE BIGGER THAN THE COUNTRY OF LUXEMBOURG!

THE BIGGEST ICEBERGS ARE NEAR THE SOUTH POLE, WHERE THEY HAVE BROKEN OFF FROM ANTARCTICA'S FROZEN COASTLINE. FOR EXAMPLE, IN EARLY 1995, A GIANT ICEBERG THAT MEASURED 23 BY 48 MILES ACROSS AND 600 FEET THICK FLOATED AWAY FROM THE LARSEN ICE SHELF. IT JOINED OTHER DRIFTING MEGABERGS THAT WERE MORE THAN TWICE THAT SIZE.

THE LARGEST ICEBERGS ARE NOW TRACKED BY SATELLITE SO THAT SHIPS WON'T RUN INTO THEM. AS OF APRIL 1996, THERE WERE AT LEAST 7 ICEBERGS NEAR THE ANTARCTIC CIRCLE THAT WERE BIGGER THAN CHICAGO.

MEGABERGS

IN THE ARCTIC, A SMALLER NUMBER OF ICEBERGS BREAK OFF FROM GLACIERS IN GREENLAND. ONE OF THESE SANK THE *TITANIC* IN 1912, KILLING MORE THAN 1,500 PEOPLE.

IT'S A FACT!

ANTARCTIC ICE IS MELTING FASTER THAN AT ANY TIME ON RECORD, CREATING EVEN MORE MEGABERGS. NO ONE KNOWS IF THIS IS DUE TO LOCAL CONDITIONS OR TO MAJOR CHANGES IN THE EARTH'S CLIMATE.

THE EARTH'S GRAVITY ISN'T THE SAME ALL OVER.

YOU WEIGH LESS ON A MOUNTAINTOP THAN AT SEA LEVEL, BECAUSE YOU'RE FARTHER FROM THE CENTER OF THE PLANET.

YOU WEIGH LESS AT THE EQUATOR THAN AT THE POLES, BECAUSE THE EARTH'S SPIN FLINGS YOU OUT FASTER THERE AGAINST THE PULL OF GRAVITY. YOU'RE LIGHTER ALSO BECAUSE THE EQUATOR BULGES YOU 13 MILES FARTHER OUT IN SPACE.

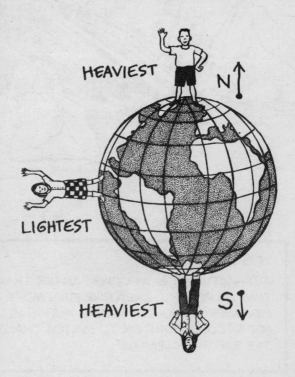

HEAVIEST

N

LIGHTEST

HEAVIEST

S

STRANGEST OF ALL, YOU WEIGH LESS WHILE STANDING OVER POROUS ROCK THAN OVER AN IRON DEPOSIT. THAT'S BECAUSE IRON IS DENSER—AND HAS MORE GRAVITY—THAN ROCK WITH A LOT OF HOLES.

IF YOU WERE ON A DIET, YOU COULD ACTUALLY LOSE WEIGHT BY MOVING TO A DIFFERENT PLACE. ACCORDING TO A GRAVITY MAP PUBLISHED BY THE U.S. GEOLOGICAL SURVEY, YOU'D WEIGH LEAST IN THE ROCKY MOUNTAINS AROUND BRECKENRIDGE, COLORADO. YOU'D WEIGH MOST IN SOUTHERN LOUISIANA, WHICH IS PARTLY BELOW SEA LEVEL. BUT DON'T COUNT ON MOVING TO CHANGE YOUR WEIGHT MUCH: THE DIFFERENCE BETWEEN YOUR HEAVIEST AND LIGHTEST WEIGHTS WOULD BE ONLY AROUND HALF AN OUNCE—ABOUT THE WEIGHT OF 6 POSTCARDS.

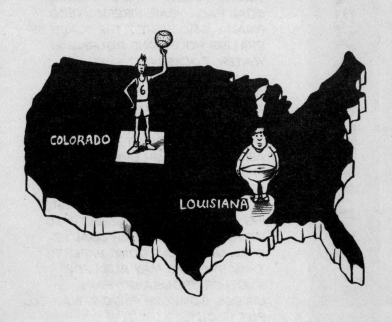

WHEN COAL IN A LARGE MINE CATCHES FIRE, IT CAN SMOLDER FOR YEARS UNTIL THE COAL OR THE AIR RUNS OUT. SUCH FIRES CAN BE HARD TO FIGHT BECAUSE AIR VENTS PULL THEM THROUGH A MAZE OF TUNNELS.

A COAL DEPOSIT IN WESTERN CHINA BURNED FOR *MORE THAN A HUNDRED YEARS,* UNTIL IT WAS PUT OUT IN 1995. THE BLAZE STARTED IN THE LATE 1800S, WHEN COAL AT THE SURFACE IGNITED. AT ONE POINT THE FIRE COVERED A 2-MILE AREA AND BURNED ABOUT 300,000 TONS OF COAL EACH YEAR. FIREFIGHTERS FINALLY SMOTHERED THE BLAZE BY DRILLING HOLES AND POURING IN WATER, ROCKS, AND SAND.

A COAL MINE UNDER CENTRALIA, PENNSYLVANIA, HAS BEEN BURNING SINCE 1962, WHEN A SMOLDERING GARBAGE DUMP SET THE MINE ABLAZE THROUGH OPENINGS ON THE SURFACE. THE FIRE QUICKLY SPREAD THROUGH THE MILES OF TUNNELS UNDER THE TOWN, FORC-ING MOST OF THE RESIDENTS TO MOVE AWAY. SO MUCH COAL IS STILL LEFT THAT SOME EXPERTS THINK THE FIRE MAY BURN FOR *ANOTHER THOUSAND YEARS* UNLESS SOMEONE FINDS A WAY TO PUT IT OUT.

YOU'VE PROBABLY HEARD OF AURORAS, THOSE EERIE CURTAINS OF LIGHT NEAR THE NORTH AND SOUTH POLES. BUT THERE ARE LESSER-KNOWN LIGHTS THAT ARE JUST AS WEIRD.

WEIRD LIGHTS

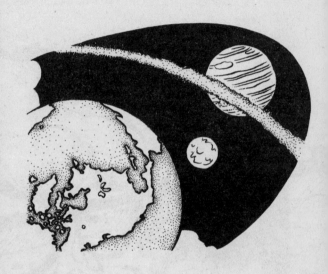

ZODIACAL LIGHT IS SOMETIMES FAINTLY VISIBLE ON THE HORIZON AFTER SUNSET. IT'S CAUSED BY SUNLIGHT BOUNCING OFF A RING OF SPACE DUST BETWEEN MARS AND JUPITER. IN THE NORTHERN HEMISPHERE, IT IS BEST SEEN IN SPRING BECAUSE THAT'S WHEN THE NORTH TIPS TOWARD THE ZODIAC—THE PATH OF THE PLANETS ACROSS THE SKY.

JUST BEFORE SUNRISE OR AFTER SUNSET, YOU CAN SOMETIMES SEE A GREEN OR BLUE FLASH ON THE HORIZON. IT HAPPENS BECAUSE THE AIR BRIEFLY ACTS AS A PRISM THAT BENDS THE BLUE-GREEN PART OF THE SUN'S SPECTRUM OVER THE HORIZON. YOU SEE IT BEST IN PLACES LIKE HAWAII, WHERE THE SUN RISES AND SETS OVER THE OCEAN.

EARTHQUAKES ARE SOMETIMES ACCOMPANIED BY GLOWING BALLS OR SHIMMERING SHEETS OF LIGHT. NO ONE KNOWS WHAT CAUSES THESE "EARTHQUAKE LIGHTS," BUT SOME THINK THEY ARE A FORM OF ELECTRICITY GENERATED BY ROCKS CRUNCHING TOGETHER (SEE "CRYSTAL POWER," PAGE 38).

EARTHQUAKE LIGHT IN SAN FRANCISCO, 1906

STRANGE THUMPS, RUMBLES, AND BOOMS ARE OCCASIONALLY HEARD IN PLACES WHERE ALL SHOULD BE QUIET.

A 300-FOOT-HIGH SAND DUNE NEAR FALLON, NEVADA, MAKES A SOUND LIKE A LOUD BASS VIOL WHEN PEOPLE WALK ON IT. IT IS ONE OF SEVERAL DESERT DUNES AROUND THE WORLD THAT MAKE ODD NOISES—INCLUDING BARKING, RUMBLING, AND "SINGING."

SOME THINK IT HAPPENS BECAUSE THE SAND GRAINS IN THESE DUNES ARE EXTREMELY SMOOTH. WHEN DISTURBED, THEY MAKE A PURE TONE THAT REVERBERATES LOUDLY.

MYSTERIOUS SOUNDS

A NOISE LIKE THE RUMBLING OF A DIESEL ENGINE OFTEN KEEPS PEOPLE AWAKE NEAR TAOS, NEW MEXICO, AND IN SOME OTHER QUIET PLACES. INVESTIGATORS HAVE BLAMED SMALL EARTHQUAKES OR SECRET MILITARY RESEARCH. BUT NO ONE HAS BEEN ABLE TO RECORD THE SOUND, AND SOME SCIENTISTS NOW THINK IT MAY COME FROM THE HEARERS' OWN EARS! IT SEEMS THAT UP TO HALF OF ALL PEOPLE GENERATE LOW SOUNDS INSIDE THEIR EARS, POSSIBLY TO HELP THEIR BRAINS FILTER AND IDENTIFY WHAT THEY'RE HEARING. IN MOST LOCATIONS, BACKGROUND NOISE FROM MACHINES AND TRAFFIC DROWNS THESE SOUNDS OUT.

AN ANNOYING HUM IN THE WATER OFF SAUSALITO, CALIFORNIA, TURNED OUT TO BE THE MATING CALL OF THOUSANDS OF VISITING TOADFISH. THE MALE FISH WERE VIBRATING GAS BLADDERS IN THEIR BODIES TO ATTRACT FEMALES.

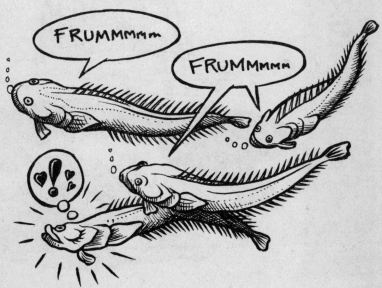

FOR HUNDREDS OF YEARS, PEOPLE HAVE OCCASIONALLY SEEN VAST NUMBERS OF CASTLES, TOWERS, COLUMNS, OR GRAZING SHEEP OFF ITALY'S STRAIT OF MESSINA. THESE THINGS APPEAR TO MOVE ACROSS THE WATER AND TO CHANGE SHAPE. SOMETIMES THEY FLOAT IN THE AIR. THIS MIRAGE BECAME KNOWN AS THE "FATA MORGANA," AFTER THE SORCERESS MORGAN LE FAY OF THE KING ARTHUR LEGENDS, WHO COULD MAKE CITIES APPEAR OUT OF THIN AIR.

MIRAGES

ITALY

BUT THE MIRAGES AREN'T CAUSED BY MAGIC. WHEN A
LAYER OF COLD AIR TRAPS HOT AIR BENEATH IT
(OR THE OTHER WAY AROUND), IT CAN MAKE THE
ATMOSPHERE ACT LIKE A MIRROR. THE SCENES
PEOPLE SEE ARE DISTORTED REFLECTIONS OF ROCKS
AND TREES ALONG THE ITALIAN COAST.

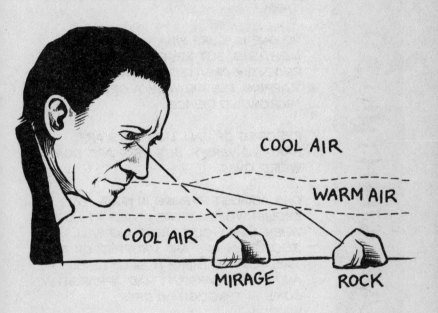

A REFLECTED SCENE IS SOMETIMES OBSERVED
FROM HUNDREDS OF MILES AWAY. IT MAY APPEAR
MAGNIFIED, DOUBLED, OR UPSIDE DOWN.

ON EXTREMELY RARE OCCASIONS, LIGHTNING FORMS A BALL SHAPE THAT MOVES AS IF IT HAS A MIND OF ITS OWN. BALL LIGHTNING HAS BEEN KNOWN TO ENTER BUILDINGS AND EVEN "CHASE" PEOPLE, GIVING THEM A PAINFUL SHOCK BUT RARELY KILLING THEM.

NO ONE IS SURE WHAT CAUSES BALL LIGHTNING, BUT RESEARCHERS RECENTLY CREATED SIMILAR BALLS BY ZAPPING THE AIR WITH A SPECIAL MICROWAVE DEVICE.

REPORTS OF BALL LIGHTNING ARE HARD TO VERIFY, BUT HERE ARE SOME WEIRD ONES.

ONE AUGUST EVENING IN 1922, TWO ENGLISHWOMEN WERE DINING AT HOME WHEN A PEA-SIZE LIGHTNING BALL ZOOMED INSIDE AND DROPPED ON THE TABLECLOTH. THERE IT SPUTTERED AND DISAPPEARED. IT HAD APPARENTLY COME IN THROUGH AN OPEN WINDOW.

THERE ARE SEVERAL STORIES OF BALL LIGHTNING MATERIALIZING THROUGH THE HULL OF AN AIRPLANE, THEN FLYING THROUGH THE CABIN AND PASSING OUTSIDE AGAIN. IN ONE CASE, THE LIGHTNING "CHASED" A FLIGHT ATTENDANT DOWN THE AISLE.

I'VE SEEN THE LIGHT!

LOOK UP IF YOU DARE—WEIRD THINGS SOMETIMES FALL FROM THE SKY!

FISH—OR EVEN FROGS AND TURTLES— SOMETIMES RAIN DOWN IN LARGE NUMBERS. SCIENTISTS THINK THAT TORNADOES SUCK THE CREATURES UP FROM NEARBY BODIES OF WATER, THEN DROP THEM TO THE GROUND.

STRANGE RAIN AND HAIL

ICE METEORS UP TO A YARD ACROSS OCCASIONALLY FALL FROM A CLEAR SKY. EXPERTS THINK THEY COULD BE GIANT HAILSTONES, OR ICE FROM THE WINGS OF PASSING AIRPLANES.

ONCE IN A WHILE, GLOBS OF WEBBY STUFF FALL FROM THE SKY. ALTHOUGH SOME PEOPLE CLAIM THEY COME FROM UFO'S, THEY ARE PROBABLY JUST WINDBLOWN SPIDERWEBS.

MOST METEORITES BURN TO DUST WITHOUT ANYONE NOTICING THEM, BUT A FEW MAKE QUITE AN IMPRESSION.

IN OCTOBER 1992, A 27-POUND METEORITE TORE THROUGH THE TRUNK OF MICHELLE KNAPP'S CHEVY MALIBU WHILE IT WAS PARKED IN HER DRIVEWAY IN PEEKSKILL, NEW YORK. A COLLECTOR PAID HER $59,000 FOR THE ROCK, WHOSE FIERY FALL HAD BEEN SEEN ACROSS THE EASTERN UNITED STATES.

IT WAS WEIRD ENOUGH WHEN A 12-OUNCE METEORITE CRASHED THROUGH THE ROOF OF A WETHERSFIELD, CONNECTICUT, HOME IN 1971. BUT IT WAS TRULY MIND-BOGGLING WHEN, 11 YEARS LATER, A 6-POUND METEORITE DROPPED ON ANOTHER WETHERSFIELD HOME LESS THAN 2 MILES AWAY! BOTH DID SLIGHT DAMAGE, BUT NO ONE WAS HURT.

OUTER SPACE MAY BE VAST, BUT IT'S NOT EMPTY. UP TO 6.5 MILLION POUNDS OF HUMAN-MADE JUNK, RANGING FROM TINY PAINT CHIPS AND ASTRONAUTS' LOST SCREWDRIVERS TO BROKEN SATELLITES, IS ORBITING THE EARTH. THERE ARE EVEN FROZEN CHUNKS OF URINE FROM THE SPACE SHUTTLE'S BATHROOM (SEE "HIGH-TECH TOILETS," PAGE 44). MILLIONS OF SUCH OBJECTS ARE WHIRLING AROUND THE EARTH AT UP TO 30,000 MILES PER HOUR, POSING A DANGER TO ASTRONAUTS.

THE SPACE SHUTTLE HAS ALREADY HAD TO CHANGE
COURSE SEVERAL TIMES TO AVOID FLYING OBJECTS,
AND ITS WINDOWS ARE OFTEN NICKED BY SMALL
PARTICLES. IF A DUST-SIZE GRAIN WERE EVER TO
PUNCTURE AN ASTRONAUT'S SUIT DURING A SPACE
WALK, HE OR SHE COULD DIE.

TO PREVENT DISASTER, TELESCOPES ON EARTH
TRACK ABOUT 8,000 OF THE LARGEST OBJECTS
SO THAT SPACECRAFT CAN STEER AROUND THEM.
ONE DAY, SPACESHIPS WILL CARRY THEIR OWN
JUNK DETECTORS. THERE MAY EVEN BE
GARBAGE-COLLECTING ROBOTS IN SPACE.

SO YOU THINK THAT'S WEIRD?

DO YOU KNOW ABOUT SOMETHING WEIRD BUT TRUE THAT BELONGS IN A FUTURE EDITION OF THIS BOOK? IF SO, WE'D LOVE TO HEAR FROM YOU! IF YOU ARE THE FIRST TO SUGGEST IT AND WE END UP USING IT, WE'LL THANK YOU BY NAME IN THE BOOK AND SEND YOU AN AUTOGRAPHED COPY. WHAT A DEAL!!

YOUR SUGGESTION MUST CONTAIN THE FOLLOWING INFORMATION—PLEASE TYPE OR PRINT CLEARLY:

• A DESCRIPTION OF THE THING AND WHY IT'S WEIRD.
• EXACTLY WHERE YOU SAW, HEARD, OR READ ABOUT IT. IF THE SOURCE WAS A NEWSPAPER, MAGAZINE, OR WEB SITE, SEND THE ENTIRE ARTICLE IF POSSIBLE. BE SURE TO NOTE WHERE IT CAME FROM AND WHEN IT APPEARED.
• YOUR NAME, ADDRESS, AND PHONE NUMBER.

MAIL SUGGESTIONS TO:
    WEIRD BUT TRUE
    P.O. BOX 31560
    SAN FRANCISCO, CA 94131

SEND AS MANY SUGGESTIONS AS YOU LIKE, BUT PLEASE NOTE THAT WE CAN'T RETURN THEM. GOOD LUCK!